OVERVIEW

Overview

Finance and accounting are at the heart of every business. Even if your role isn't directly focused on finance, your activities have financial implications. Understanding how money flows through your organization empowers you to make better decisions and identify profitable solutions. In this course, you'll learn about basic accounting concepts and principles and walk through the four-step accounting process. You'll also learn the fundamental principles of cash flow management and cover the four types of financial risk.

It's not only the folks in the finance department who have to plan and monitor budgets. It's actually in everyone's best interest to have some basic budgetary knowledge. In this course, you'll learn about planning an effective budget, the stages involved, and different types of budgets. You'll also be introduced to Historical and Zero-based budgeting, variance analysis, capital budgeting, and performing budgeting calculations.

Sorin Dumitrascu

To maintain your company's finances, you need a handle on the Income Statement, Cash Flow Statement, and Balance Sheet. And if you want to improve your company's finances, financial statements will hint at problems and possible solutions. This course will give you an overview of the three statements. You'll learn which items are included in each statement, how the statements are interlinked, and what each one indicates about your company's financial position.

Financial analysis helps you understand your organization's financial standing, how it got there, and its strengths and weaknesses. In this course, you'll learn about the concept of the Time Value of Money as well as the methods for analyzing financial statements from a non-financial professional's perspective. These methods include using profitability ratios for analysis; analyzing Efficiency Ratios; Liquidity Ratio analysis; analyzing Solvency Ratios; and Vertical and Horizontal analysis.

CHAPTER 1 - Basic Accounting Concepts for Non-financial Professionals

CHAPTER 1 - Basic Accounting Concepts for Non-financial Professionals

The Basic Accounting Equation
Cash-based and Accrual-based Accounting
Understanding the Accounting Process
Basic Accounting Principles
Cash Flow Principles
The Impact of Economic Float on Cash Flow
Working with Capital to Increase Cash Flow
Negating Financial Risk Like a Pro

The Basic Accounting Equation

The Basic Accounting Equation

Accounting is best left to accountants, right? Actually, that's not true. All non-financial professionals stand to benefit from a firm grasp of basic accounting concepts. Being able to back up your business proposals, projects, and ideas with numbers puts you in a stronger position. As does being able to recognize the financial value of your work – how you contribute to the bottom line. Okay fair enough, so what is accounting? Accounting mostly deals with transactions that have taken place and data that's been recorded. Beyond recording transactions and maintaining them, it also includes preparing, presenting, and interpreting financial information.

The best place to start is with the basic accounting equation – the founding principle of accounting. It's used to determine the figures you need to understand the viability and health of a business. The accounting equation is: assets equals liabilities plus owner's equity. So we're dealing with three things: assets, liabilities, and owner's equity.

Assets are the "things" owned by a business. These take many forms – cash, money that's due from customers – known as accounts receivable. Then there's also equipment, land, buildings, inventories, patents, copyrights, and investments. Liabilities are the financial obligations the business owes to outside entities. Some examples are money owed to suppliers, loans, mortgages, interest, taxes, and payroll owed but not yet paid. The last element – Owner's equity – is the financial interest of the business's owners. It's the claim the owners, partners, or stockholders have against the business assets. For an incorporated business, the term "stockholders' equity" is used.

For accounting purposes, the most important thing is to keep the equation in balance. If someone pays you what they owe, for example, that amount must be removed from where it says you're still owed X amount; and vice versa. So let's say your company borrows $50,000 from the bank to buy materials. The assets side of the business must show the $50,000 you now have, while the liabilities side – what you owe the bank, in this case – must show $50,000 as well to balance it out.

You can also invert the equation to calculate owner's equity. The formula to do that, is: assets minus liabilities. Let's consider a simple example to see how this works. A small delivery business has a bank balance of $20,000. The company owns a truck valued at $7,000, so the business assets are $27,000. It has $2,000 in as-yet-unpaid payroll and it's also paying off a long-term start-up loan of

$15,000. So the company's liabilities add up to $17,000. To calculate owner's equity, you use the equation – assets minus liabilities. In this case, owner's equity would be $27,000 minus $17,000, which equals $10,000. Understanding how transactions like these affect your organization will improve your business acumen.

Cash-based and Accrual-based Accounting

Cash-based and Accrual-based Accounting

One of the first financial tasks for any business is to decide how to do the books. Say you've just opened a new business and you're unsure whether you need a professional accountant or if you can get manage without one. You're also unsure when to log income – when you deliver goods, or when customers actually pay for them? What you need, is to choose between the two basic accounting types – Cash-based or Accrual-based.

So let's start with the simpler of the two – Cash-based accounting. Its focus is on keeping track of cash inflow and outflow. It's ideal for an individual or small business that really just wants to cover the basics for tax purposes. In this case, a journal of cash receipts and expenditures for the year – such as a well- maintained checkbook – is usually sufficient.

But most businesses need more robust information about their assets and liabilities than that. Cash-based accounting won't cut it if your business sells or buys on credit and if you carry inventory – which most businesses do. Or perhaps you need to invest in long-term operating assets, or make long-term commitments, like employee pensions.

In that case, Accrual-based accounting is your best bet. This method records sales revenue – money you get when products are sold – when products or services are delivered to the customer. It's not concerned about when exactly the customer makes payment, because you assume the customer will pay what they owe. So sales revenue is often recorded before money is actually received. Likewise, expenses are recorded as soon as you buy something – even if the money hasn't left the business account yet.

The fundamental difference between the two accounting types is the time a transaction is recorded. In accrual-based accounting a transaction is recorded when it happens, even if no cash is involved. In cash-based accounting, a transaction is recorded when cash changes hands. So the two methods measure the annual revenue and expenses of a business quite differently.

Let's say your business uses cash-based accounting. Within a week of the end of its fiscal year, you make a $10,000 sale on 30-day terms. The sale would go on the following year's records. But if you made the same sale using accrual-based accounting, the $10,000 would be recorded in the current fiscal year.

The two approaches also differ in how they measure annual profit. With cash-based accounting, profit is calculated as the difference between cash inflows from sales and cash outflows for expenses. If there's an increase in cash after expenses – that's the profit. Accrual-based accounting is more complex and considers other factors. Cost of goods, for example, is not calculated as an expense until products are sold. It also considers the depreciation of assets, money invested in the business by its owners, and accumulated profits.

Make sure you understand the benefits and drawbacks of each accounting type before committing to one.

Understanding the Accounting Process

Understanding the Accounting Process

Do you understand the accounting process? To avoid accounting errors, you need to be able to work methodically. Luckily, there are various phases to guide you.

The first phase of accounting – Analysis – is about analyzing and understanding each transaction. Before recording anything, ask yourself what type of transaction you're dealing with – debit or credit? Which accounts will it affect, and how? For example, say you're starting an online store and you buy a web server for $10,000. You pay for it out of your business checking account, so the cash account must be credited. The equipment account – which is an asset – increased, so it must be debited. For balance, the accounts on the assets side of the equation – the cash assets and the long-term assets – are respectively credited and debited by $10,000 each.

The second phase – Recording – has two important levels: journalizing and posting to the ledger. Journalizing is simply a record of the day-to-day debits and credits in one or more journals. Journals – also referred to as "books of original entry" – are where all transactions are noted first. The various journal entries are then sorted into their appropriate accounts and posted to the ledger.

The ledger is the book of final entry, and final accounts and financial statements are prepared based on this. It contains a company's various accounts, such as Cash, Account(s) Receivable, Equipment, Accumulated Depreciation, Account(s) Payable, Sales, Expenses, and so on. Information is extracted from the ledger to prepare various financial statements. One such statement is the Cash Flow Statement – it shows the movement of cash in operating, investing, and financing activities, and indicates the net increase or decrease in cash during a period.

Adjusting, the third phase of the accounting process, is usually performed by the accountant. It involves adjusting entries to ensure the business's financial situation is accurately reflected. It's an important step that happens in each accounting period. A typical adjustment, for instance, is recognizing the reduction in the value of an asset – its depreciation – through use or consumption. The principle of the basic accounting equation also applies. So an adjusting entry that shows a decrease in an asset's value must also show a corresponding increase in liability. And that needs to happen by the end of the accounting period. To do this, you use a Balance Sheet – which reports the Assets, Liabilities, and Owners' Equity of a company at a point in time.

The fourth and final phase of the accounting process is Closing. At the end of the accounting period, accounts are balanced out. This is done via the Income Statement – a record that summarizes the company's profit or loss for a given period. During closing, the revenue and expense sides of the Income Statement are actually "closed." The new opening balance starts at zero.

The phases in the accounting process helps you determine which accounting activities to perform, and when.

Basic Accounting Principles

Basic Accounting Principles

Accounting procedures and standards are subjective. What we mean by that, is it's up to you to decide which approach works best for your business. But to start, you need to understand the underlying principles that help shape the various accounting methods.

The first principle – Money Measurement – evaluates a business based only on monetary characteristics, such as gross profit, net profit, and cash on hand. It's convenient because all businesses have this basis in common. You can calculate the net profit of a child's lemonade stand and a multi- billion dollar international corporation, and very quickly compare the two. But it's particularly useful when comparing similar businesses. There's one severe limitation, though. Many of the most valuable business assets, such as copyrights and brand names, are intangible. And those aren't easily measured in terms of money.

The next principle – Business Entity – only considers a transaction's effect on the business. It's not interested in how a transaction affects the people involved. Business Entity is useful if you've a smaller business where transactions affect you and the business differently. Say you own a restaurant that's going through a quiet period. You put $15,000 of your own money into the business to keep its doors open. Applying this principle would mean only recording that the business has $15,000 more to work with. The effect on you personally is quite different – you're $15,000 out of pocket. But this isn't a consideration when using this principle.

Next is the Going Concern principle. It's based on the assumption that a business will be successful in the long run. This outlook affects the way the accounting method valuates business assets and costs. Think about it. If you aren't planning on selling your business assets in the near future, you don't have to be overly concerned with accurately evaluating them.

But say you do want to calculate an asset's value. Should you base it on its current market value or what it would cost to replace it? Both are subjective. That's why the fourth principle, Cost Concept, records an asset's value in terms of its original cost. It's an easy and objective value to work with. When the Cost Concept is applied together with the Going Concern Principle, it simplifies the accountant's job. There's no need to speculate on an asset's value – just record what it originally cost.

Finally, the Realization principle focuses on when revenue should be recorded. Let's say you manufacture toasters. When should you record the revenue for the sale of a toaster – once it's sold, once it ships to the distributor, or once final payment is received? According to this principle, revenue is realized when goods or services are provided. So in this case, it should be recorded when the items are delivered to the buyer.

You can decide which principles are most convenient and effective for shaping your business's accounting procedure.

Cash Flow Principles

Cash Flow Principles

Money might make the world go round. But it's not much use if you don't have it when you need it! Cash, however, is money you can access. And it's vital to the operation of every business.

Businesses get cash by selling their products and services. And when sales don't provide enough cash, they rely on additional resources called Cash equivalents – safe short-term securities that can be converted to cash relatively quickly. In other words, they're "liquid" assets. Bonds with short maturity dates or money market funds, for example.

When you sell a product or service, or cash in on an investment, cash flows into the business. And it flows out when you purchase raw materials and equipment, pay salaries and taxes, repay loans, and make investments.

This in-and-out may sound seamless – but in reality cash flow needs to be carefully managed.

That's if you want to always have enough cash on hand to meet obligations and unforeseen expenses. Especially when you consider that cash outflow and inflow happens at different times. You might deliver a product today and only receive payment 30 to 90 days later. That sort of time lag can create stress on your business and lead to a cash deficit.

All cash flow falls under one of three activities. Operating activities are transactions that affect income and expenses. Cash flows in from the sale of products or services, and other non-sales incomes. And cash flows out to buy inventory, pay employees and taxes, and so on. Let's say you own an advertising agency. Your operating activities could include cash inflow from clients paying for advertising services; and cash outflow to pay salaries, make payments to suppliers, and pay insurance premiums.

Next, Investing activities are transactions that affect things owned by the business – the assets – as well as securities like stocks and bonds. These include cash inflow and outflow from buying and selling land, buildings, plants, equipment, operating divisions, securities, or other assets. If your advertising agency took out a loan a year ago to upgrade your employees' computers, for example, your monthly repayments would be an investing activity.

And finally, there are Financing activities. These are transactions that affect the owner's equity and long-term creditors. Cash flows in from borrowing cash on a short-term basis and from investments made by the owner.

And cash flows out to cover withdrawals, to repay loans, or to buy some of the company's own stock. Suppose your agency's bid for a citywide ad campaign is successful and you want to expand the business. To afford an additional ten employees and the lease on a new building, you decide to publicly trade in company-issued stock on the market. That would be a financing activity.

Cash is the lifeblood of a business. To manage it effectively for your day-to-day operations, you must understand how it's received and distributed.

The Impact of Economic Float on Cash Flow

The Impact of Economic Float on Cash Flow

Ever been frustrated, waiting for a check to clear? Well then you've experienced float. It's the status given to funds in transit. The name comes from the idea of money floating around before arriving at its final destination. Businesses usually have large amounts of funds in float. As useful as it may be, it can have a negative effect on cash flow if you don't use it correctly.

Economic or total business float is the time between when a sales order is received and the customer's cash for that order is made available. Of course, delays occur at various stages during the sales process. And these individual periods of float all add up to make the economic float. Some delays are unavoidable but others can be shortened. So how does this work in practice?

Let's say you operate a nursery that wholesales plants and trees to florists and landscape companies. Business is booming, but you're still sometimes strapped for cash. To try and figure out why, you decide to map out your sales process. As it turns out, excess float is slowing your cash flow down at various stages. Let's look at some examples.

The first delay happens between when you receive a sales order and when goods are delivered to the customer. This is called production float. In this case it's prolonged, because you used to accumulate orders and only submit them to the warehouse once a week. To fix this, you now submit orders three times a week.

Another delay occurs between when the customer receives their invoice and when the invoice is filed for payment. This is credit float, and it's causing a big holdup. If you send invoices to clients via the post, that can take days. Each mail has to be sorted in the mail room and sent to the customer's mailbox. And then the customer still has to send it on to accounts payable. To speed things up, you send invoices via e-mail. That way you cut out all mail and handling delays.

Removing excess float saves time, which in turn saves money. In fact, you can roughly calculate the potential cash gained from speeding up your cash flow. All you need is your annual sales volume and the number of days of float you can cut out. Say the nursery makes $750,000 per year and you manage to eliminate seven days of float. To begin, divide your sales volume – $750,000 – by 365. The result – $2,054.79 – shows the impact a single day of float has on your cash flow. Next, multiply this by the number of days of float you aim to remove – seven. The outcome – $14,383.53 – is the potential cash gain you'll achieve by removing float.

If you remove the holdups in your sales process, this will optimize your cash flow and make your money work harder for you.

Working with Capital to Increase Cash Flow

Working with Capital to Increase Cash Flow

If you think you might be coming down with a cold or the 'flu, checking your temperature is a good place to start. But what's the best way to check the health of your business? The answer – check your working capital: the amount of cash available to run the business on a daily basis.

You can calculate capital by subtracting short-term liabilities from current assets. So really, it all comes down to cash flow. When there's enough working capital, cash flow is good and day-to-day expenses – like buying inventory or paying bills – are easily covered. But when working capital falls too low, you'll know all about it. Cash flow is poor and it's a struggle to just get by. If times are tight and you're strapped for cash, there are three key areas to focus on.

The first – inventory – includes your raw materials, work in progress, and finished goods for sale. If you don't manage inventory carefully, it can swallow up a lot of cash. Your goal is to only buy what's needed, when it's needed. Otherwise you could end up with excess inventory collecting dust in warehouses.

Say, for instance, you pay for a large shipment of timber for your furniture business. After meeting your sales orders, you realize there's a lot of timber left over. That's cash that could have been spent more productively. If you reduce your inventory, cash is released back into your cash flow. This also cuts down on storage-related expenses, like rent, electricity, and insurance.

The next factor to consider is accounts receivable – the debts owed to you by your customers. This is typically the main source of income for a business. When customers fail to pay bills on time, they withhold cash. You may be counting on that cash to settle your own accounts or buy stock. So it's critical to monitor accounts receivable and encourage customers to pay their bills quickly. You could offer a discount for payments made within 15 days of invoicing. Or if a customer exceeds their 30-day payment window, you could call them immediately to follow up. This would shrink accounts receivable to make more cash available.

Finally, there's accounts payable – your credit available from banks and suppliers. Buying things on credit improves your cash flow. That's because you get what you need, without spending your money. But when you pay bills in cash, there's less cash available for your use. So aim to postpone payment for as long as possible and increase your accounts payable.

For example, if you run a construction firm, you could negotiate a 90-day payment cycle with your suppliers. This gives you ample time to buy materials on credit and hold onto your cash for three months – this helps increase your cash flow.

To revitalize your working capital, find ways to reduce inventory and accounts receivable or increase accounts payable.

Negating Financial Risk Like a Pro

Negating Financial Risk Like a Pro

It's easy to recognize the risks involved in extreme sports like skydiving or snowboarding. But when it comes to investments, the risks are often less obvious. If you're going to gamble, it's best to know what the odds of winning and losing are. Otherwise you might bite off more than you can chew. There are several types of risk to consider when making financial decisions.

The first – default risk – is the likelihood you won't be able to get your money back or receive the return you're owed. Most investments are subject to some amount of default risk but it varies greatly. A new startup company, for instance, has a much higher chance of defaulting than a well-established global corporation. If the new company's product or service doesn't catch on, investors may lose their entire investment.

Next, inflation risk is the chance of there being a predictable increase in prices for goods and services; which devalues an investment over time. This isn't much of a problem for short-term investments. But for investments over longer periods, yearly inflation rates can take their toll and eat away at the initial investment sum and its return. You may want to set a threshold for the level of inflation risk you're comfortable with.

When you tie up your money in an investment with a set period, you expose yourself to the third risk type – maturity risk. It's the possibility that you'll miss out on more profitable opportunities while waiting for your investment to mature. Again, time is a major factor – because the longer your money's stuck in an investment, the more opportunities may present themselves. This isn't something you can really predict, but it's worth considering. Should you rather wait for a better opportunity, or should you invest in something short-term?

Liquidity risk – the final risk type – is the possibility that you may need to sell your investment to free up cash. So you have money to invest now – but what if something changes and you need to get it back? First find out whether selling is an option. If not, the time period of the investment is a serious factor to consider. If you could sell, find out whether there's enough demand on the market to fetch a reasonable price. Government bonds, for example, almost always have a ready market. But there might not be enough buyers interested in speculating on a startup venture to make a quick stock sale.

So you'll do well to determine what level of risk you're comfortable taking – by reviewing the relationship between the overall amount of risk and the potential rewards.

CHAPTER 2 - Basic Budgeting for Non-financial Professionals

CHAPTER 2 - Basic Budgeting for Non-financial Professionals

Attributes of an Effective Budget
Planning a Budget
Sales, Production, and Cash Budgets
Historical Budgeting
Zero-based Budgeting
Budgetary Variance Analysis
Capital Budgeting
Performing Budget Calculations

Attributes of an Effective Budget

Attributes of an Effective Budget

Many organizations have a clear idea of what position they wish to be in financially, but lack a realistic plan to get there. This is where the budget comes in. Simply put, a budget is a document that outlines how an organization's financial resources are allocated to specific activities.

But is creating a budget really that important? Well, it can benefit an organization to know how money will be spent. This, in turn, makes it possible to plan where funds go ahead of time. Budgetary planning also motivates different departments to coordinate with one another. This coordination helps ensure everyone is realistic about how much funding they can expect. Another benefit is that budgeting encourages interdepartmental collaboration when it comes to production activities.

Basically, it's a good way to – literally – get everyone on the same page.

Unfortunately, sticking to a budget is often perceived negatively. Employees may view it as the company trying to micro-manage their every move. If large amounts of money are allocated to certain departments, this may seem like favoritism.

As you can imagine, this may lead to interdepartmental conflict. If employees associate how much – or how little! – money their department receives with how much they're valued, managers may not want to keep accurate records. This can cause inflated budgets.

Then there are inflated egos – some managers may feel the need to request more money than they actually need, to appear important. This is a great waste of money and such a budget will be ineffective. At this point you may be asking yourself what exactly, then, would make an "effective" budget.

Well, a truly effective budget relies on various elements and strategies. One of these strategies is to involve key individuals from various departments during the planning stages. These people may have valuable insight and perspectives that you may not have considered. Encouraging broad participation across all departments helps reduce the risk of employees being unhappy with the final budget.

Another characteristic of an effective budget is that it defines business goals in quantifiable terms – in other words, the outcomes such as time and money spent, must be measurable. If your budget provides quantifiable data, it will be easier to monitor financial progress on a regular basis.

Because circumstances can change very quickly, an effective budget should be able to adapt to whatever happens. There should be enough flexibility in your budget to take advantage of opportunities and respond to obstacles that are bound to pop up.

Taking the time to create an effective budget is one of the most important contributions you can make to the success of any business.

Planning a Budget

Planning a Budget
When planning a budget, it may be tempting to rush through it so you can get going with the project. However, budgetary planning is not a race – it's a journey. And there are some very important stops you have to make along the way. Your planning process needs to go through a few crucial phases if you want your budget to be effective in the long run.

So where do you start? Well, the first phase in planning your budget involves figuring out where the goalposts are – the strategic objectives you're aiming for. Those need to be nailed down first. And to do that, you need to know in what direction the business is headed – by asking senior executives questions about the company's goals, weaknesses and strengths, if you need to.

For example, if there's been a change in safety regulations, a company that manufactures car seats may want to ramp up production to meet the new requirements. So their budget would need to reflect these new strategic goals.

Okay, so you know where you're headed, financially. But you can't get there alone. So for the next phase in planning the budget, you need to get input from the relevant people to decide how business activities will be performed. It may be useful to set specific targets. But remember, for targets to be realistic, you should consult the key players in the organization.

So for the car seat manufacturer, this could mean determining the number of car seats they aim to produce and sell during each financial quarter. And they'll establish which extra activities may need to be performed by various departments to reach that target.

Once the targets and activities are defined, the next phase in the process is estimating the resources you need. When we say resources, we mean not only money, but also time from employees and materials.

In the example of the manufacturing company, this may mean getting rough estimates on how much upholstery, fiberglass, and so on they would need to produce their target number of car seats. This may also include calculating whether extra personnel may need to be recruited for a particular production period.

After completing the estimation phase, it's time to move on to the last phase – providing each department with a detailed budget. This is where things may get tricky. You may need to do some careful negotiation to keep everyone happy. The budget may also need to be amended a few times before it's finalized. But once the details have been agreed upon by all parties concerned, the Master Budget can be created. The Master Budget then serves as the company's "financial road map" – to control and monitor the progress of projects.

To ensure you end up with an effective Master Budget, it is in your best interest to be thorough in each of the phases of budgetary planning.

Sales, Production, and Cash Budgets

Sales, Production, and Cash Budgets

Keeping track of finances for the various departments within an organization, can be tricky. This is why having a well-designed Master Budget is so important. The Master Budget is a container for the different functional budgets created during the budget planning process.

These include the sales, production and cash budgets. The Master Budget may also contain others – the administration budget, the research and development budget, and the capital budget.

But let's not get ahead of ourselves. What do we mean when we talk about "functional budgets?"

The sales budget is one of the most common functional budgets. You'll usually prepare the sales budget first, since its content may impact other budgets. It contains two types of information: the estimated sales volume – the number of items you predict you'll sell – and the projected sales income – how much the business will earn as a result. Information in the sales budget can be organized according to quarters, seasons, or regions.

Once you've done the sales budget, you create your production budget. This budget helps ensure the company produces a sufficient number of units to support the total sales you're aiming for, as outlined in the sales budget.

So a production budget essentially outlines how many units need to be produced in a particular budget period. To determine the number of units to be produced, you need to know three values – the estimated sales volume, the beginning inventory, and the desired ending inventory.

To start calculating the number of units to produce, you add the estimated sales volume – as defined in the sales budget – to the desired ending inventory. And because there may be some inventory left over from the previous budget period – known as the beginning inventory – you subtract this from the calculated number of units to determine the actual number of units required.

Aside from the sales budget's objectives, your production budget also needs to consider other factors – your factory's capacity, the direction of stock movement, as well as outside purchases.

Once the production budget is done, you create the cash budget. A cash budget gives you an overview of how cash flows in and out of your business during a specified period.

Cash outflows can include things like wages and loan repayments, while cash inflows typically involve sales of goods or services. Your cash budget will also stipulate how much cash you have on hand at the start of the budget period, and how much – if any – you'll have left over at the end of the period.

You can estimate the ending cash balance by adding the beginning cash on hand to the inflow; then you subtract the cash outflow from that amount.

The Master Budget summarizes all the functional budgets, thereby providing a global view of all the budgetary information. While these budgets may vary, the sales, production, and cash budgets are the ones you'll most likely be dealing with.

Historical Budgeting

Historical Budgeting

It can seem daunting to prepare a budget. You need to make lots of important decisions, after all. One of the most important of these, is which budgeting method you're going to use.

There are two commonly-used approaches: Historical budgeting and Zero-based budgeting. While these two can be used individually just fine, they can also be used together. But deciding which approach to use, is up to you.

"Historical budgeting" means using a previous budget as basis for creating a new one. It's also sometimes referred to as Traditional or Incremental budgeting. Because you use an existing budget as a starting point, and just tweak it a little, this approach relies on the assumption that the organization's strategy hasn't changed from budgeting period to another. However, in reality, this is rarely the case.

But on the positive side, it will save time and money, since you won't need to start a budget from scratch. Also, because you're using a budget that's been applied before, you'll know what works and what doesn't.

Let's consider the example of a company that manufactures work clothing. The company has a ten-year contract with another manufacturer as the sole supplier of their workwear. Now in the sixth year of the contract, none of the original terms have changed. So a Historical budgeting approach may be ideal in this instance, since unexpected changes are very unlikely. Also, since this approach saves time and money, resources can be spent in other areas where they are needed more.

The biggest disadvantage of the Historical budgeting approach, however, is that it does not allow you to deal with change effectively. In the ever-changing business landscape, relying on the assumption that everything will remain the same is risky. The truth is that your economic circumstances and organizational focus may change at any time. The approach also doesn't allow for regular opportunities to rethink the status quo. Reviewing a budget can give you the opportunity to rethink your business goals and find ways to improve the way you work. But if you're merely recycling budgets, this type of analysis and rework is not bound to happen.

Imagine, if you will, what may happen if your budgeting approach can't adapt to a change in regulations or any other part of how you conduct business. If your budget is set in stone, another supplier could take a long-standing customer away from you.

Sorin Dumitrascu

Because effective budgeting governs the success of any business, you need an approach that works. The Historical budgeting approach can save you time and money, but its lack of flexibility is a consideration.

Zero-based Budgeting

Zero-based Budgeting

Crunching the numbers for a budget is not always an easy task. To ensure the budget you're planning is effective, you can use one of two approaches – Historical budgeting or Zero-based budgeting. These two are standalone, but can be used together – if you understand the difference between them and the pros and cons of each approach.

The Zero-based budgeting approach is simple – you start the budget from scratch, or point zero.

When using this approach, you need to be able to justify the effectiveness and necessity of each activity before it's accepted into the budget. This compels you, or any other budget planner, to reconsider the value of activities. You may need to come up with alternative solutions to any problems you encounter. The main benefit of using Zero-based budgeting is that it encourages innovation – you consider change and allow for flexibility. Instead of passively accepting the current way of planning a budget, you adopt a questioning attitude. You re-evaluate each outlined activity and approach it from a fresh perspective. Zero-based budgeting assumes nothing and questions everything. By following this type of approach, you may come up with new and innovative solutions to old problems.

Of course, Zero-based budgeting also has a downside. The two main disadvantages are – it can be time consuming and costly. Starting each budget from scratch and reevaluating every activity, will inevitably take up a great amount of time, manpower, and resources. So it's advisable to run a cost-benefits analysis before deciding on this approach. It may turn out not to be worth the cost, in which case you should consider a different approach.

You could consider using Zero-based budgeting in conjunction with Historical budgeting. By using Zero-based budgeting periodically, and relying on Historical budgeting in the interim, for example. Or you can decide to only use Historical budgeting in the more predictable areas – where procedures are well regulated, for instance, such as in the banking sector – and apply Zero-based budgeting in departments such as R&D where more innovation is needed.

When considering using the Zero-based budgeting approach, you'll be wise to consider its pros and cons before you decide if it suits your organization's needs.

Budgetary Variance Analysis

Budgetary Variance Analysis

Any budget involves a certain amount of speculation and guesswork, and there may be some miscalculations. So how can you ensure that your costs and revenues won't come in much higher or lower than calculated? Unfortunately I can't predict the future, but there are various analytical tools that may help. One such tool is budgetary variance analysis.

So what exactly does "variance" refer to? Simply put, a budget variance is the difference between the amount you budgeted for, and the actual amount. Because life hardly ever goes according to plan, actual results will often differ from what you planned for in your budget.

Variances can be positive or negative. Negative variances are sometimes referred to as "adverse variances," while positive variances are also referred to as "favorable variances."

If actual results are less than what you budgeted for – that's negative variance. This can happen for many reasons, including cost overruns, increased tax liabilities, or a drop in sales.

A positive variance, on the other hand, is when the actual results exceed what you forecast in the budget. This can happen if tax rates or expenses are reduced, or if you have an unexpected surge in sales.

To check whether your budget sets realistic goals, you need to run a variance analysis and review the reports you get as a result, at regular intervals. If there are positive or negative variances – big or small – you need to know about them ASAP. You can then decide if they're worth investigating and make changes if you need to.

A variance report reveals the difference between the financial outcome planned in your budget, and the actual outcome. The report usually displays the budget year, the budget items being monitored, the actual results, the planned results, and the variance. The variance can be displayed as an amount or as a percentage value.

Variances are more likely in some budget items than others. Budget items like direct wages, cost of materials, and overheads, for instance, should always be included in your variance reports.

However, not all variances are significant enough to be cause for worry. If you were to investigate each and every variance, that may be a waste of time and manpower. Luckily, there are criteria to help you decide whether to investigate variance or not. You should consider things like size, whether the variance is positive or negative, the likelihood of it happening again, and its controllability.

The size of any variance is probably the most important factor to consider. You need to ask yourself if the size of the variance is large enough to be cause for concern. If a variance is particularly large, you might want to consider running reports more often.

So to stay on track in reaching your financial goals, monitoring any variances in your budget is great – allowing you to monitor progress and make adjustments as necessary.

Capital Budgeting

Capital Budgeting

When making investment decisions, always remember to "look before your leap." And that's where capital budgeting comes in.

Capital budgeting is a "blanket term" for all the different ways to assess if an investment is a good one. Basically, you use it to figure out whether an investment is likely to be worth your money by being profitable.

One capital budgeting method is the Payback Period, or PP. It focuses on how long it will take a company to recover the amount it's investing. The PP method is typically used to screen potential investments. It's fairly simple to understand and calculate – it lets you do a quick comparison between various investments based on their payback period.

To calculate the payback period, you divide the initial investment by the cash flow. Generally, the shorter the payback period, the less risk is involved. And less risk means a better investment.

One drawback of the PP method is it doesn't consider the company's cash flow after the payback period. Nor does it consider the changing value of money over time. So the PP method is best used with other capital budgeting methods.

Another method for capital budgeting is the Net Present Value, or NPV. The NPV is the present value of all expected cash flows combined. To calculate NPV, you subtract the total present value of investments from the total present value of returns. Basically, a positive NPV means a good investment.

The NPV method is great for comparing mutually exclusive projects. But it's sensitive to discount rates and time periods.

Another method you can use to appraise investments, is the Internal Rate of Return, or IRR. An investment's IRR value is the interest rate that brings NPV to zero. Basically, the IRR method indicates the breakeven rate at which your cash inflows and outflows will be equal. As a general rule of thumb – the higher the IRR, the better the investment.

To calculate IRR, you divide the net cash flow by the sum of one, plus the rate of return, raised to the power of time. In this equation, net cash flow is represented as the acronym NCF, the rate of return is lowercase r, and the time value is lowercase letter t. But if, like me, you're not a big fan of calculations – the IRR formula is built as a function into most spreadsheet applications.

IRR is easy to interpret, considers cash flows, and provides you with objective data.

Unfortunately, it isn't foolproof. It assumes the interest rate will not change throughout a project's life span. Another disadvantage is that it won't work in projects where the cost of capital changes or if an investment has fluctuating cash flows. IRR calculations also tend to rely on NPV calculations.

Choosing between investment proposals can be tricky, but with the help of capital budgeting methods it doesn't have to be a leap of faith.

Performing Budget Calculations

Performing Budget Calculations

Choosing the best investment for your company can be tricky. Sure, they may all seem promising, but which one will yield a profit? The only way to be sure, is to use suitable capital budgeting methods.

The Payback Period, or PP, method evaluates risk based on the amount of time – the payback period – it takes a company to recover the money it's invested. This method's ideal when sifting through investment options – use it as a preliminary screening to narrow down your options.

Because all projects differ, there are typically two types of payback periods: those with even cash inflows, and those with uneven cash inflows. Simply put, a project could have a constant inflow of cash; or cash may come in at odd times throughout the year.

If your project has an even cash inflow, to calculate the payback period – PP – you divide the net investment by the annual cash inflow. Pretty straightforward.

If, however, a project has an uneven cash inflow, things are trickier. You first need to determine how many cash flows you'll need to get your initial investment back.

Consider, for example, a project with a net investment of $30,000. Since the total revenue after three years is only $28,500, the investment will be returned during the fourth year. So to calculate the amount that's returned in the fourth year, you subtract the total of the first three years from the total investment. In this case, that's $30,000 minus $28,500, which gives you $1,500.

But when in the fourth year will this amount be returned? To calculate this, you divide the payback amount by that year's cash inflow – in this case that's $1,500 divided by $5,000, which is 0.3. To get the payback period, you add 0.3 to the three years. And voilà. It will take 3.3 years for your investment to be returned.

Another method used in capital budgeting is Net Present Value, or NPV. When comparing the profitability of mutually exclusive investments, this is your best bet. This method factors in that the value of money is likely to change over a period of time. So it measures the value of different cash flows at the present point in time.

Once you've calculated the NPV, it's very easy to decide whether to accept or reject the proposal. If the NPV is larger than zero, it's a go; if it is less than zero, it's a no.

Calculating the NPV is done in three steps. First, you calculate the present value of the expected returns. Then you calculate the total present value of investments. You then subtract the total present value of investments from the total present value of returns to get the NPV.

You then repeat the process to get the NPV for each investment you want to compare.

Using PP and NPV methods to perform budget calculations, can help you make solid investment decisions.

CHAPTER 3 - Comprehending Financials - A Guide to Financial Statements

CHAPTER 3 - Comprehending Financials - A Guide to Financial Statements

Deconstructing the Income Statement
Performing Calculations Using the Income Statement
Managing Cash Flow
Deconstructing the Cash Flow Statement
Using the Cash Flow Statement
What You Need to Know about Balance Sheets
Compiling the Balance Sheet
Connecting the Dots: Financial Statements in Action

Deconstructing the Income Statement

Deconstructing the Income Statement

Though you might find it a hassle to figure out financial statements, understanding them prevents mistakes that could seriously affect your company's financial position.

You're probably familiar with the Cash Flow Statement, Balance Sheet, and Income Statement. Each one is important, but for now, let's zoom in on the Income Statement. The Income Statement looks at a certain period, usually a year, and tells you if your company has made a profit, and by how much. It calculates how much money your company has taken in – mainly revenue from sales – against expenses. Some businesses call it a Profit and Loss Statement or Earnings Statement. Others call it the Statement of Activities or the Statement of Operations.

There are many people who want to, or need to, look at your company's Income Statement. Business professionals, like managers, investors, and analysts use it in their work. Creditors need it to assess your company. Lastly, government and regulatory agencies may require the information and usually you have to comply when they request the statements.

So what does everyone want to check for in your Income Statement for? Mainly, to get to grips with the breakdown of your company's net income – also called the net profit or more commonly, the "bottom line." Anyone reading an Income Statement will find a standard layout with two main parts.

First, it states net sales or revenue and subtracts direct production costs to get the gross profit. The gross profit is a tally of all the money your company has made for the period the Income Statement covers. In the Income Statement, direct production costs are called "cost of goods sold." Also to actually make a gross profit, you need to sell products or services for more than it costs to make them. In the second section of the Income Statement, you'll find the net profit. To calculate the net profit, business expenses, which are the running expenses of your company, and any applicable taxes are added together. This value is then subtracted from the gross profit. The net profit is called "net income" on the Income Statement. And if your company's expenses are more than its gross profit – your company has made a net loss, rather than a net profit

In some instances an Income Statement might also include a section for other income. This is for items such as investment income or interest income.

So the Income Statement is a necessary tool to confirm if, and by how much, your company has made a profit.

Performing Calculations Using the Income Statement

Performing Calculations Using the Income Statement

Your company can't plan ahead without knowing whether it's made a profit or not. That's one reason for producing an Income Statement – it gives your company direction.

An Income Statement comes in two formats. The simpler form is the single-step format, which uses just a single subtraction. Let's say, a business's revenue totals $109,083, expenses and any losses are $90,394, with a tax provision amount of $15,458. Then you subtract – revenue less your expenses and tax equals a net income of $3,231 – simple, that's your Income Statement.

The more complex multi-step format includes several calculations. This format combines your company's operating and non-operating activities and categorizes different expenses. The advantage – you can compare the

Incomes Statement better and it's more complete. It also helps with analyzing and checking profitability.

Let's examine a multi-step Income Statement. You'll notice its split over three sections. And there are three main steps to reach the net profit.

Revenue is for total sales – the money earned through the sale of services or products. You subtract returns and allowances from total sales to get the net revenue.

The first section is Cost of Goods Sold, which is also called cost of revenue. Here you state the amount spent to produce goods or services, for example, on raw materials and labor. You'll also include any adjustments for inventory.

Deducting the cost of goods sold from the net revenue gives you the gross profit – the profit made after accounting for the cost of goods sold. For example, if your net revenue is $21,485,536 and you deduct the cost of goods sold, which is $12,314,024, your gross profit is $9,171,512. This is step one to calculate the net profit.

The next section is operating expenses. These are indirect or general expenses that any company needs to run itself, like advertising or office supplies.

When you deduct the operating expenses from the gross profit you get the income from operations, also known as operating profit. For example, if you deduct operating expenses of $5,361,054 from your gross profit, your income from operations is $3,810,458. Now you've completed step two.

The third section, Other Income and expenses, follows. Here you'll put non-primary activities of the business, like investment interest and stock compensation. Include a provisional tax amount if necessary.

Now you can calculate the net income, also called the net profit or "bottom line." This gives the profitability over the period covered by the Income Statement. To finish the example, you'll take the income from operations and deduct the total of other income and expenses and tax to get a net income of $2,189,833. This is the final step to get the net profit.

Following these three steps means you can calculate your net profit on the Income Statement and assess how your business has made its profit.

Managing Cash Flow

Managing Cash Flow

If your company's ever faced being cash strapped, it's probably a consequence of cash flow not being managed strategically.

But what is cash flow? It's the flow of cash into and out of your company. When your customers pay their bills there's an inflow. Outflow takes various forms – the accounts manager holds onto funds for daily expenses and emergencies; or money is used for investments, debt, and spent on growing the company. While the basic principle is to maximize inflows and minimize outflows, you can use four basic strategies to strategically manage cash flow.

First up – managing credit – this helps your company's growth and financial stability. But extending credit does come with a risk. With the right client it can increase sales. Cash flow is stimulated and cash moves into the business quickly. But, with high-risk clients or on the wrong terms, it can discourage payment. You end up losing business and can't meet profit goals. So a measured credit policy based around your company's products and services is essential. It must be flexible and help you reach your profit goals.

Most company's credit policies probably have a turnaround period of, say 30 or 60 days, for accounts receivable. But employing techniques for collecting cash quickly, can ensure that payments are received when they are due or sooner. A credit policy could offer discounts off bills paid early or discourage delayed payments. Issue a finance charge if bills are unpaid after a certain date. And reduce the billing window by billing as early as possible. Consider billing large orders bit by bit to avoid waiting before an entire order is filled to submit an invoice. Also, use electronic billing and collections to save time and avoid mail float.

If you want to hold onto your money, delaying payments is a strategy that does exactly that – you delay paying bills as long as possible. This involves prioritizing invoices and scheduling them for payment. Also, schedule mailings to gain maximum delay and use company credit cards to avoid paying for smaller items immediately.

The last strategy, monitoring costs and inventory, is useful for companies who spend a lot on overheads. Consider appointing consultants in place of employees to save on benefits costs. You can save money by outsourcing accounting or customer support functions. Cut office space expenditure by consolidating personnel and equipment and moving into cheaper space. Consider renting office space instead of buying. Or selling property that you already own.

Sorin Dumitrascu

If you company holds inventory, keeping it as low as possible means less money spent on suppliers and storage. Review inventory to reduce parts not in demand or unsold. And consolidate inventory in fewer locations and rent out unused buildings. Finally, monitor your suppliers' prices and negotiate the lowest prices and most favorable terms.

Fine-tuning and using these strategies in your company will significantly reduce the risk of cash flow shortages.

Deconstructing the Cash Flow Statement

Deconstructing the Cash Flow Statement

Though your company's Income Statement may reflect a profit, that doesn't mean it has enough cash to pay for expenses like materials and wages – that's information you'd find in a Cash Flow Statement.

This is important information for managers so they know if there's money to pay bills. Investors monitor your Cash Flow Statement to check whether you're making enough money. And financial professionals want to check if your company can pay creditors.

So what exactly is the Cash Flow Statement? It's a document of your company's cash inflows and outflows for a certain period. Your company's profitability – calculated in the Income Statement – and cash flows are closely related. The revenue and expenses you'll find in the Income Statement will eventually convert into cash inflows and outflows. Besides profitability, you also need to consider liquidity, or how much cash or cash equivalents your company's assets hold. Because profit measures all transactions, even those yet to be paid or collected; your company's ability to pay bills and fund regular operations is tied to its liquid assets. Or, simply, how much cash you have.

Put another way, the Cash Flow Statement and the Income Statement differ based on the accrual accounting system. The Cash Flow Statement lists actual cash moving through the business. But the Income Statement's revenue and expenses aren't necessarily cash transactions.

The two statements also differ because an Income Statement subtracts non-cash expenses, like depreciation, to get the net income. The Cash Flow Statement adds these amounts back to reflect the actual amount of cash the business has. It also factors in changes in assets and liabilities. So increases in liabilities or decreases in assets increases cash; while increases in assets or decreases in liabilities decreases cash.

Let's examine the layout of the Cash Flow Statement. Information is split in three sections. Each section is totaled and added to Cash at the Beginning of the Year to calculate net cash.

The operating activities section lists the net income and adjustments for assets and liabilities. It'll include the general business activities such as stock compensation and changes in accounts payable. Interest payments and taxes, as well as accounts receivable from the previous period are added here.

The investing activities section follows. This is for fixed assets adjustments – think property and equipment. Included here are discretionary investments – items your company purchases that eventually will generate cash, like buying or selling capital assets; as well as land or property. If your company invests in bonds or receives dividends from owning stocks, that information goes here.

And the last section, financing activities, lists adjustments for sharing cash with owners or investors – creditors would also apply. It includes financial items, like taking out or repaying loans. If you receive or issue stock it'll be noted here. Also, paying dividends to shareholders must be included here. Understanding the different parts of the Cash Flow Statement will let you know what's relevant to each section.

Using the Cash Flow Statement

Using the Cash Flow Statement

Whether your company is cash strapped or cash rich, calculating the Cash Flow Statement will confirm if you have enough cash to pay expenses, as well as where to find extra money.

So let's prepare a Cash Flow Statement. First you'll need to complete operating activities. This section includes your company's net income, which you'll get from the Income Statement. Next you'll add line items for depreciation and amortization. You'll also need to account for deferred income tax.

Then you'll add items related to changes in assets and liabilities since the last statement period. These may include accounts receivable, inventories, or other assets. You'd also include accounts payable, income taxes receivable and payable, as well as restricted stock compensation. Lastly, other accrued liabilities also go here. Add these all up to get net cash from operating activities.

Then you list the information for investing activities. This includes adjustments involving fixed assets, say, your company sold or leased equipment or spent money on fixed assets – it goes here. You'll add these up to get the net cash from investing activities.

The last section you'll complete is financing activities, which relates to managing money. Items here include credit payments and proceeds from term loans. Also, if your company has long-term debt, development grants, and stock options, include it here. Record the repurchase of common stock and principal payments on long-term debt. Lastly, any excess tax benefits of options and restricted stock goes here. Then add these up to get the net cash from financing activities.

Once you've added the totals for operating, investing, and financing activities, you can work out the net cash for the period of the Cash Flow Statement. This total gives the net increase or decrease in cash or cash equivalents. But it's unlikely that you started the financial period with zero cash. So add in the net cash and cash equivalents amount from the previous period's Cash Flow Statement. This you'll find on the last line of the previous period's Cash Flow Statement. Finally, this gives you the total net cash amount for the covered period.

Your Cash Flow Statement will tell you which transactions affect your company's cash flow. Accounts receivable are sales which haven't been paid for. Your accounts payable is how much your company still owes suppliers and creditors. Inventory, on the other hand, is where money is tied up in making or purchasing inventory. In each area you can find ways to bring cash into the business.

So the Cash Flow Statement is a vital snapshot of how well your company is prepared for paying expenses. It also offers clues on where in the business that money might be held.

What You Need to Know about Balance Sheets

What You Need to Know about Balance Sheets

Your company could end up in a vulnerable financial position if decision-makers don't have a clear idea of how financial transactions affect the company's standing.

An overview of your company's financial position can be found in the Balance Sheet. It checks the assets owned by the company against the liabilities due and the equity of shareholders. Generally your accountant will draw up the Balance Sheet using the basic accounting equation – assets equal owner's equity plus liability. The value of assets must always equal liabilities plus equities. From your owners' or shareholders' view, value is a question of how equity measures up against assets less outstanding liabilities – as in what their share in the company is worth.

With an Income Statement or Cash Flow Statement, you're looking at changes over a set period. A Balance Sheet, however, covers a certain point in time of your company's financial position. It's what your company owes and owns at any given point. Because of this, you need to know how different types of transactions affect the Balance Sheet.

A Balance Sheet is divided into Assets and Liabilities. The Asset section is divided into four categories. Cash on hand is money available for general business purposes. Any short-term obligations that your customers owe your company – that's receivables. Then you have inventory on hand, which covers your raw materials and any work in process. If you have finished goods or goods purchased for resale, they will be listed here. The last category is net PP&E – property, plant, and equipment – which are long-term operating assets.

On the Liabilities side of the Balance Sheet, is a listing of the liabilities and owner's equity. Liabilities include operating liabilities, such as utility bills. These are short-term and do not bear interest, unlike interest-bearing liabilities, such as bank loans. Owner's equity includes owner's invested capital – the money owners initially invested and any further investments. You then have owner's retained earnings – the profits earned and retained by the business.

The layout of the Balance Sheet makes it easier to visualize the equation – assets equal equity plus liability. Consider this your company's perspective because assets, from where your company gets its value, are either purchased with debt, so a liability is created, or they belong to your owners or shareholders. Remember that the Balance Sheet always has to balance. Any changes in assets must match a change in the liabilities/equity ratio to keep the equation in check.

So if your company takes a $500,000 bank loan at 5% interest to buy equipment, certain items in the Balance Sheet will shift. Assets will increase because your company now has more equipment. On the other side, liabilities will increase because your company has to pay back a loan with interest. In this way, the Balance Sheet balances out with each transaction.

If you have a clear understanding of how transactions affect your company's financial position, your financial decision-making will be enhanced.

Compiling the Balance Sheet

Compiling the Balance Sheet

The task of completing a Balance Sheet can be daunting, but it's treated as an authority on your company's financial position. And various parties will check it and use it in their decision-making.

If you understand the credo, assets equal owner's equity plus liability – that is the basis on which you'll develop your Balance Sheet. Your company's completed Income Statement and Cash Flow Statement will also come in handy.

So let's start with the asset side of the Balance Sheet. You'll have sections for Current Assets and Fixed Assets. Current Assets, which some call Liquid Assets, can be converted into cash without affecting your day-to-day business immediately. Fixed Assets, on the other hand, can't be converted into cash so easily. It refers to what your company needs in order to produce its products and services.

First off, from the Cash Flow Statement, you'll need the net cash amount, from the last line of the statement. List this amount as Cash, under Current Assets. You'll also add accounts receivable and doubtful accounts, which will be a negative figure. Inventory, short-term investment, and prepaid expenses also go here. Add these up to get your total for Current Assets.

Then under Fixed Assets you'll include long-term investments as well as amounts for copyrights and patents. This will also include items like land and buildings as well as equipment, furniture, and fixtures. Then for each fixed asset, you subtract the accumulated depreciation. Once the accumulated depreciation is subtracted, add these all up to get your total for Fixed Assets. You'll add this amount to the total for Current Assets to get the final total for Assets.

Let's move to the other side of the Balance Sheet, the Liabilities. Here you separate Current Liabilities from Long-term Liabilities. Current liabilities are debts or obligations your company has to clear in one year. Long-term liabilities, however, won't be cleared in the current fiscal year. The Current Liabilities will include items like accounts payable and short-term notes, as well as the current portion of long-term notes. You'll also add interest payable, taxes payable, and last, accrued payroll, should also go here. Add this all up.

Long-term liabilities include two items – the mortgage and other long-term liabilities. These two amounts are added together to give you a total for Long-term liabilities.

Now you calculate the Owner's Equity. Depending on how your company's set up, you might need information from the Income Statement to complete this. If yours is a publicly traded company, insert the Shareholders' Equity. Then add the two totals for Current Liabilities and Long-term Liabilities to the Owner's Equity. The test of accuracy is that this amount has to match the total for Assets. This confirms the Balance Sheet is in order.

Completing the Balance Sheet means you can get an immediate view of where the company stands financially.

Connecting the Dots: Financial Statements in Action

Connecting the Dots: Financial Statements in Action

A financial transaction causes ripple effects across the Income Statement, Cash Flow Statement, and Balance Sheet. If you're aware of the possible impact a financial decision can have, you can influence decisions to protect the business's financial position.

Have you ever had to examine the impact of financial decisions on your company? Or perhaps looked into what financial options your company has? Most likely, you'd have looked up the relevant Income Statement or Cash Flow Statement, perhaps the Balance Sheet as well. But to get a complete picture of a company's financial state, you need to examine all three of these documents. They are interconnected financial perspectives of your company, for whatever period they cover.

Sorin Dumitrascu

Each statement has a function. An Income Statement tells you how much profit, if any, your company has made over a certain period. If you want to check how much cash has moved into and out of the company for a certain period, the Cash Flow Statement gives that information. And then the Balance Sheet gives the financial status of your company for a specific point in time. Your assets are balanced against liabilities and owner's equity.

These documents are different windows or perspectives of the same company. If any changes happen in your company, each document will reflect the ripple effects because they are interlinked – the same financial data is used for each of them. Think about how information flows in these documents. The net income amount which you calculate in the Income Statement is used to get the retained earnings in the Balance Sheet. And it's also part of operating activities in the Cash Flow Statement. Likewise, the net cash amount that you calculate in the Cash Flow Statement for the end of the period is used in the Balance Sheet as the cash asset under current assets. This means the Balance Sheet gets information from both the Income Statement and Cash Flow Statement.

Let's take a closer look at how one transaction affects all the financial statements. Suppose you sold goods to the value of $1,000. This is a cash sale. So on the Income Statement revenue will increase by $1,000, which ups net income as well. On the Cash Flow Statement, the net cash amount will increase by $1,000. Your Balance Sheet will shift on either side by a $1,000. On the Asset side, net cash will increase, which is taken from the Cash Flow Statement. On the Liabilities/Owner's Equity side, Owner's Equity's retained earnings will increase by

$1,000, which is taken from net income in the Income Statement. You still have a balanced Balance Sheet.

Each transaction has its own dynamic that plays out on the statements. And with various transactions taking place at any given time, having a broader perspective of the impact on the company's financial position, means you can influence decisions for the better.

CHAPTER 4 - Financial Statement Analysis for Non-financial Professionals

CHAPTER 4 - Financial Statement Analysis for Non-financial Professionals

- The Time Value of Money
- Present Value and Future Value Calculations
- Using Profitability Ratios for Analysis
- Analyzing Efficiency Ratios
- Liquidity Ratio Analysis
- Analyzing Solvency Ratios
- Horizontal Analysis
- Vertical Analysis

The Time Value of Money

The Time Value of Money

Imagine you've been given a choice: you can either receive $25,000 in lottery winnings now or four years from now. Most people would probably say, "I want it now." It's almost always better to have money now instead of later because prices can increase and money can lose its value and purchasing power over time.

Right, now you have the money to spend. But...what if you want to save it instead? You can't keep it under your mattress. But if you know about the time value of money, you can figure out the best way, from several options, to make your money grow.

One of these options is investment, which is using money or capital to purchase financial assets in order to gain profitable returns. You may have been in a situation where you had to decide which possible investment option was the best. However, because the value of money changes over time it's impossible to compare, for example, cash flows that occur at different times.

To account for money changing value over time, the value that two or more amounts would have at the same point in time is calculated. You can either calculate the future value of an investment or calculate the present value of an amount to be received in the future.

The return on your investment is subject to factors such as the principal (p), which is the amount invested. Then consider the interest, or the cost a person or institution pays to use someone else's money. It's generally added to the amount invested at regular intervals. The interest rate (i) is expressed as an annual percentage of the principal. A final consideration is the period of time(n), which is the number of years your money is invested for.

As a consumer, you've probably heard about inflation. Inflation is the rate at which the lender is compensated for the possible loss of an investment's value, or purchasing power, over time. Take the example of a company considering an investment that offers a 4% return. They must account for the current estimated inflation rate of 6% per year. The minimum rate of return on the investment must be high enough to make it worthwhile. In this case, inflation may end up costing the company money.

An annuity is another savings option. Annuities are a series of fixed payments at a specified frequency over the course of a fixed period of time. Annuities are calculated in a similar way to single amount future and present values. In the case of future value, an annuity is the sum of all the payments plus the accumulated compound interest on them. When you calculate an annuity's future value, you need to know the interest rate, the number of compounding periods, and the amount of the periodic payments. Now that you're familiar with the time value of money, you can choose the best way to make your money grow.

Present Value and Future Value Calculations

Present Value and Future Value Calculations

At some point, you, like most people, will need to predict how the outcome of a particular financial decision will affect you. Interest, future value, present value – all play a key role in determining where your money should go. But, before any interest or future value calculations can be done, the values for principal (p), interest rate (i), and time (n) are required. Forecasting is essential for making informed investment decisions. To get started with forecasting investment opportunities, you need to know two things. First, the present value – the value right now of an investment that is to be received at a future date. For example, the present value of $1,000 is $1,000. Investing it will make it grow depending upon the amount of time and the interest rate. The second is the future value – the value of a single amount at a specific future date after it has been invested, with compound interest added.

When calculating future and present values, notice the relationship between them. Looking closely, you'll notice that for the future value of a single amount, the present value is one of the key components of the formula. Future value is equal to the present value – the principal invested – multiplied by the sum of 1 plus i, which is then raised to the power of n. "i" is the interest rate for the period, and "n" represents the number of periods for which the interest will be added.

Let's try this. If you have $25,000 invested at an interest rate of 4%, or percentage fraction 0.04, for three years – you will end up with a value of 1.125. This value is called the Future Value Interest Factor (FVIF). When you multiply $25,000 by 1.125, you get a future value of $28,125.

Forecasting means looking forward to predict the future. But suppose you already know what your goal is and you want to know how much to invest now to reach that future goal. In a sense you'll calculate backwards to get the present value. Present value is equal to the future value multiplied by the result of the following equation: one, divided by the sum of one plus i to the power of n.

The Present Value Interest Factor (PVIF) and the FVIF are available from a PVIF table that is freely downloadable off the Internet. Let's say you need $12,000 in two years. The interest rate is 5% and you want to find out the present value, or simply, how much to invest now. You begin by checking these numbers against the PVIF table to obtain the PVIF rate. In this case, it's 0.907. To get the present value you multiply $12,000 by 0.907. This gives you $10,884. So if you need $12,000 in two years and the interest rate is 5%, you'd need to invest $10,884 today.

So understanding present and future value calculations will help you to make the investment choice that best suits your needs.

Using Profitability Ratios for Analysis

Using Profitability Ratios for Analysis

It's safe to say that without profitability, a business wouldn't survive in the long run. Profitability ratios help you determine if a company has the ability to earn a profit in the future. It includes Net Profit Margin, Return on Assets, and Return on Equity and uses elements of both Income Statements and Balance Sheets.

The Net Profit Margin ratio – also known as Profit Margin on Sales or Return on Sales (ROS) – measures how well a company can turn sales into net income. It measures management's success in controlling costs and pricing and tells you the net profit per sales dollar after all expenses are deducted from the total sales amount.

To calculate the Net Profit Margin you divide Net Income by net Sales. Although a high profit margin is generally better than a low profit margin, this value shouldn't be analyzed in isolation. It needs to be compared to ratios from previous years, to ratios of other companies in the same industry, or to an accepted reference value. Sometimes a low profit margin is just a part of doing business in a specific industry sector.

Take a company with a net income of $1.45 million and sales of $23.4 million. If you divide $1.45 million by $23.4 million and multiply by 100, the result is a 6.2% Net Profit Margin. This means that the company earns a profit of $6.20 for each $100.00 of sales revenue.

However any company can show a profit. So for more clarity let's use another profitability ratio: the Return on Assets (ROA). ROA measures how well a company uses its assets to generate net income. So it indicates which businesses can make good profits with little assets.

It's calculated as Net Income divided by Total Assets. This formula measures how much profit, after taxes, was earned on the total capital contributed by creditors and owners. So like Net Profit Margin, the higher the ROA, the better. So if a business has earned $375,000 in net income on $2,500,000 in assets. The ROA would be $375,000 divided by $2,500,000, which is 0.015. As a percentage the ROA is 15%.

The next ratio is Return on Equity (ROE), which measures the return shareholders are receiving on their investment in the company. It lets shareholders gauge management's ability to return money for each dollar they've invested. You can use this ratio to compare the profitability of different companies in the same industry.

The formula is Net Income divided by Shareholders' Equity. As with the other profitability ratios, the general rule for ROE is that higher is better. Shareholders' Equity includes both capital stock and retained earnings. So a

Net Income of $2,189,833 divided by a shareholders' equity of $7,670,217 would result in 0.28549, or 28.55 %.

Profitability ratios help you to determine if a business is able to generate profits from assets, equity, and sales to ensure its long term survival.

Analyzing Efficiency Ratios

Analyzing Efficiency Ratios

When investing in a business, you're definitely hoping it's profitable and a return will be coming your way. But in your analysis of a company's financial status, give efficiency ratios some room at the table as well. They're used for measuring management's effectiveness in managing assets and liabilities to generate revenues and profits. To calculate efficiency ratios, you use information from Income Statements, Cash Flow Statements, and Balance Sheets.

You'll get the most benefit from using efficiency ratios, when you use them to compare businesses in the same industry. The first efficiency ratio is Receivables Turnover ratio, which measures how many times a company's accounts receivable turn over in a period – typically one year. When companies extend credit to clients, it results in accounts receivable.

So how's it calculated? You divide Net Credit Sales for the year by the Average Accounts Receivable for the year. Only credit sales should be included in the net sales figure. Generally, a higher receivables turnover is better, since that means there's a shorter time to collect. A simple evaluation is for management to take the average number of days taken by customers to pay debts and compare it to the number of days in the credit terms. For example, an average collection period of 33.46 days would indicate good efficiency for payment terms of 45 days for credit sales.

The second ratio is the Inventory Turnover ratio, which measures the number of times a company sells and replaces its inventory in a given period. It indicates how fast a company can sell its goods. And is useful because it helps manage "frozen cash", which is cash invested in in-process and finished inventories.

It's calculated with the formula Cost of Goods Sold (COGS) divided by the Average Inventory. The higher the turnover, the better. The goal is for the Inventory Turnover Ratio to increase over time so that there's less investment in stock. The turnover rate should be high enough that cash can come in from customers before suppliers need to be paid.

The third ratio is the Operating Cash Flow to Sales Ratio, which gives you an idea of a company's efficiency in turning sales into cash. It's expressed as a percentage and shows the relationship between cash generated from operations and sales made over a specified period. Operating cash flow is the net cash generated from operations, which includes both net income and changes in working capital. It's found on the Cash Flow Statement.

The formula used is Operating Cash Flow divided by Net Sales which is found on the Income Statement.

Cash is just as important as profit because a company needs cash to pay dividends, suppliers, and creditors, and to purchase assets. The higher the Operating Cash Flow to Sales Ratio, the better. After all, a company's sales and operating cash flow should grow in parallel.

Efficiency ratios let you analyze the efficiency of a company's management of resources and investments.

Liquidity Ratio Analysis

Liquidity Ratio Analysis

Liquidity brings to mind the idea of flowing water. In finance, liquidity means having cash, as well as the ability to quickly convert assets into cash. For a business this means cash flows freely enough so it can pay off its current liabilities quickly with what it has. Liquidity ratios, which are sometimes called working capital ratios measure the availability of cash.

When thinking about liquidity, you should also consider solvency. Solvency is all about business risk. For example, the inability of business to pay off debts and investments from its assets and cash flow on a long-term. Both liquidity and solvency ratios use elements of the Balance Sheet: a statement of financial position, which gives a snapshot of a company at a given point in time. It typically lists assets, liabilities, and capital.

Liquidity ratios measure the short-term solvency of a business; gauging the company's ability to meet its credit obligations. There are two commonly used liquidity ratios.

The Current ratio expresses how well a company is able to pay its creditors from its current assets. As one of the best-known measures of financial strength, it answers the question "Are there are enough current assets to meet the current liabilities with a margin of safety?" It's worth mentioning that current assets are assumed to be convertible into cash within one year, and current liabilities are short-term debts that are due in one year or less.

The formula is Current Assets divided by Current Liabilities. In general, a Current ratio of around 2.0 is good for a lender or creditor. Higher or lower values might be a cause for concern.

You know that the Current ratio includes all Current Assets. The Acid Test ratio includes only the most liquid current assets. It's also called the Quick ratio because it only includes cash and current assets that can quickly be converted to cash. It's more accurate in measuring true liquidity because it doesn't include inventory and prepaid expenses. This ratio answers the question, "If all sales income were to stop, could the business still meet its current obligations with the quickly convertible funds it has on hand?"

It's calculated with the formula Liquid Assets divided by Current Liabilities. Liquid assets are cash, marketable securities, and accounts receivable. As a rough guide, the Acid Test ratio should be 1.0 or higher. When the ratio is 1.0, it means that liquid assets are pretty much equal to the liabilities owed. So the company can pay what it owes without needing to sell its inventory.

But what does it mean if it is less than 1.0? Possibly the company isn't solvent for the short term. But, in some industries, 0.7 might be acceptable. These companies have liquid assets available to cover just less than three quarters of the current liabilities.

So a company that is highly liquid inspires confidence as their short term financial situation is secure.

Analyzing Solvency Ratios

It takes hard work to pay off debts for both businesses and individuals. In financial terms, solvency means being able to pay all legal debts even if you have to convert assets to cash. Basically, debts can be dissolved by the assets. Liquidity ratios relate to what's currently happening. But solvency ratios take a longer-term approach and help you determine if a company is financially overextended. There are two commonly used Solvency ratios, which both use elements of the Balance Sheet.

The first one – Debt to Total Assets – includes both short-term and long-term debt as well as tangible and intangible assets. It's calculated by adding up the company's Total Debt and then dividing by Total Assets. This ratio measures the percentage of assets financed by creditors, as opposed to the percentage financed by owners. It gives you an idea of a company's ability to withstand losses while still being able to cover its obligations.

A high Debt to Total Assets ratio might be a red flag that the business may not be able to meet its long- term obligations. This business might be called highly debt leveraged. A ratio under 1.0 means that most assets are financed through equity and earnings, while a ratio above 1.0 means they're financed more by debt.

For example, total liabilities of $110,000 divided by Total Assets of $200,000 gives you a ratio of 0.55. This isn't bad –about half of the company's assets are financed through equity. But it could also indicate a conservative approach to opportunities of leveraging on potentially low interest debts.

The Debt to Equity ratio on the other hand compares debt to owners' equity instead of comparing debt to assets. When you calculate how much the company is leveraged in debt, you can find the relationship between what is owed and what is owned.

The shareholders' – or owners' – equity is the claim stockholders have to a company's assets once all creditors and debtors have been paid. It's the company's net worth, and it's calculated by subtracting total liabilities from total assets. The Debt to Equity ratio is the tool that highlights the extent to which debt is covered by shareholders' funds

The formula for the Debt To Equity ratio is Total Liabilities divided by Total Shareholders' Equity. Sometimes, only interest-bearing, long-term debts are considered instead of total liabilities in the calculation. For example a Total Liabilities of $110,000 divided by the

Total Shareholders' Equity of $90,000 results in a ratio of 1.22. This is a relatively high ratio.

As a rule of thumb, a high Debt to Equity ratio may indicate high risks – such as interest rate increases and creditor nervousness – and even financial weakness. The company may have been too aggressive in financing its growth with debt.

You can now use the power of solvency ratios to check whether a company's longer-term obligations can be met easily or not.

Horizontal Analysis

Horizontal Analysis

Let's face it – it's not always easy to interpret all the figures in financial statements based on their values alone. [A sample Balance Sheet is displayed.] For instance, can we say that a company with a liability of $20,000 is less exposed to risk compared to another company with liabilities of $200,000? Not really. The riskiness depends in part on the size of the company and how much it has in assets. And also on the nature of each company's business.

When dollar amounts vary greatly, it's difficult to compare the performance of two companies. Even evaluating the performance of one company over time becomes harder. To remedy this, you can use horizontal and vertical analysis of financial statements. Very cleverly, these types of analyses use dollar amounts converted to percentages. A vertical analysis expresses each item as a percent of a base amount.

But a horizontal, comparative, or trend analysis, is the process of examining how specific items in a financial statement vary over time. Think of when you compare financial information for two or more years, you follow a single line item – such as sales revenue – in a straight line across each year's statements.

As well as checking actual dollar amounts, it lets you compute percentage changes from year to year for all balances. Because it looks at trends over years, it helps spot areas of divergence that can alert you to problems or changes.

It's helpful to look at industry averages as these give you an idea of what values are normal and acceptable. So to perform horizontal analysis and highlight trends–whether positive or negative – you take a base year as a reference and calculate how other years vary from it.

After selecting the base year, you calculate the percentage of variance from the base year's data. First, you set consecutive Balance Sheets, Income Statements, or Cash Flow Statements side-by-side, and look out for any changes. Then you restate the amounts of each item, or group of items, as a percentage of the base year amount. The base year figures will always be 100%, and the changes from the base year expressed in relationship to that.

Suppose you're reviewing inventory from year 3 of a business. Year 3 is the base year. Year 1's inventory of $121,000 is divided by Year 3's inventory of $83,000 to get a percentage of 146%. This indicates that the amount of inventory at the end of Year 1 was 146% of the amount it was at the end of Year 3. Year 2's inventory of $100,000 is also divided by Year 3's inventory of $83,000 to get a percentage of 120%. So inventory is 120% of the base year at the end of Year 2. This allows you to examine how each item has changed in relationship to the changes in other items.

Now you can use horizontal analysis to examine financial statements and check what has changed over time.

Vertical Analysis

Vertical Analysis

Trying to compare data from companies that differed in size used to be an absolute nightmare. Luckily for us vertical analysis became our savior. Just as in horizontal analysis, all of the amounts are converted into percentages. The difference lies in what pieces of data are set as 100%.

In vertical analysis, the items given base values of 100% are the most important pieces of financial data. Everything else gets converted to percentages of those items. Just like that, size isn't an issue anymore. And the relative composition of assets, total liabilities and equity, and revenues and expenses is revealed. Both Income Statements and Balance Sheets can be analyzed in this way. Depending on the source document, the percentage figures result in the output of a common-size Balance Sheet or common-size Income Statement.

For a vertical analysis of a Balance Sheet, total assets are set as the base value, and every other asset is expressed as a percentage of it. The total liabilities and equity amount is also assigned 100%, and each liability and shareholders' equity account is expressed as a percentage. In the Income Statement, net sales is the base value having 100%.

The vertical analysis of a Balance Sheet shows how assets, liabilities, and equity are related. For example – what mix of assets generates income? What mix is from financing? Whether by liabilities or by equity. What percentage of total assets is inventory? What happens if that percentage changes significantly? What mix of various expenses a company has incurred? What percentage of total assets is made up of equity? What percentage is from liabilities? And what percentage of total assets comes from accounts receivable?

Vertical analysis calculations let you examine the composition of each of the elements on a financial statement. For an Income Statement, it reveals how many cents of each sales dollar are absorbed by various expenses. For example, if expenses in a company equal 57.3% of total net sales, it means for every $1 in sales earned, more than 57 cents goes to the costs of goods sold.

The vertical analysis of multiple years of financial statements can help you determine if significant changes have occurred. Similarly, you can also compare between financial statement items in companies of different sizes. The first step is to transform a given year's balance sheet amounts into percentages of total assets and total liabilities. When the calculations are complete for all years, the sum of the percentages for the individual asset accounts needs to equal 100%. Then, because assets equal total liabilities plus equity, the sum of the percentages for the various liability and equity accounts will also equal 100%. It's more meaningful when the percentages are compared with competitors', or industry averages - or over a longer period of time for one company.

Using vertical analysis you can make certain financial comparisons between companies, regardless of size or dollar amounts.

www.ingramcontent.com/pod-product-compliance
Lightning Source LLC
Chambersburg PA
CBHW020926180526
45163CB00007B/2900